SPOTLIGHT ON

RENAISSANCE EUROPE

Nathaniel Harris

SPOTLIGHT ON HISTORY

Spotlight on the Age of Exploration and Discovery
Spotlight on the Age of Revolution
Spotlight on the Agricultural Revolution
Spotlight on the Cold War
Spotlight on the Collapse of Empires
Spotlight on Elizabethan England
Spotlight on the English Civil War
Spotlight on the First World War
Spotlight on the Industrial Revolution
Spotlight on Industry in the Twentieth Century
Spotlight on Medieval Europe
Spotlight on Post-War Europe
Spotlight on the Reformation
Spotlight on Renaissance Europe
Spotlight on the Rise of Modern China
Spotlight on the Russian Revolution
Spotlight on the Second World War
Spotlight on the Victorians

Cover illustration: The Marriage of Giovanni Arnolfi and Giovanna Cenami by Jan van Eyck

First published in 1986 by Wayland (Publishers) Ltd
61 Western Road, Hove, East Sussex, BN3 1JD, England

British Library Cataloguing in Publication Data
Harris, Nathaniel
    Spotlight on Renaissance Europe.—(Spotlight on history)
    1. Europe—History—1492–1648—Juvenile literature
    I. Title   II. Series   940.2′1   D228

ISBN 0 85078 653 3

Typeset, printed and bound in the UK by The Bath Press, Avon

CONTENTS

1 The Waning of the Middle Ages   4

2 The Renaissance in Italy   11

3 European Power-Struggles   22

4 Reformation and Counter-Reformation   32

5 The Art of War   41

6 Literature and the Arts   48

7 Social and Economic Life   62

Date Chart   71

Glossary   72

Further Reading   74

Index   75

1 THE WANING OF THE MIDDLE AGES

'**R**enaissance' is a French word, meaning 'rebirth', which describes a great general movement that began in Italy and then very gradually spread north of the Alps. The Renaissance transformed politics, warfare, society, the arts and everyday life. Behind these visible changes was a set of new human attitudes and interests that were responsible for them. Renaissance men and women thought differently about themselves and their world, and therefore behaved differently, from the men and women of the Middle Ages. The Renaissance became the bridge between two worlds, the medieval and the modern; its first great historian, Jacob Burckhardt, a Swiss, wrote of it as 'a civilization which is the mother of our own, and whose influence is still at work among us'.

In Italy the new attitudes were forming as early as the fourteenth century, when gifted individuals such as the painter Giotto and the poet Petrarch introduced the Renaissance in the arts. Renaissance ideas began to reach other countries in the fifteenth century, but it is only in the sixteenth century that we can reasonably speak of a 'Renaissance Europe', which had unmistakeably emerged from the Middle Ages. The new Europe was not just a product of Italian ideas, since each country altered them to suit its own traditions. Other powerful influences, such as nationalism, religious differences, and the discovery of new lands, were also at work.

The Renaissance Europe of the sixteenth century is the main subject of this book. But to understand it properly we must look briefly at the old world it replaced.

The medieval outlook
Like most societies, medieval Europe was not a uniform or even a consistent 'system'; and it undoubtedly altered over the centuries. Nevertheless there are certain features that can be identified as medieval, and which had disappeared by 1600.

Medieval society was based on the ownership and cultivation of land. Trade and manufactures existed, but it was rare for them to be of more than marginal importance. The feudal system arranged this society as a hierarchy, with the king at the apex of a pyramid which descended through great barons, lords of the manor and other owners,

The excitement and atmosphere of the European Renaissance is preserved in paintings such as this one by Raphael.

The fourteenth-century poet Petrarch was one of the first to introduce Renaissance ideas in the arts.

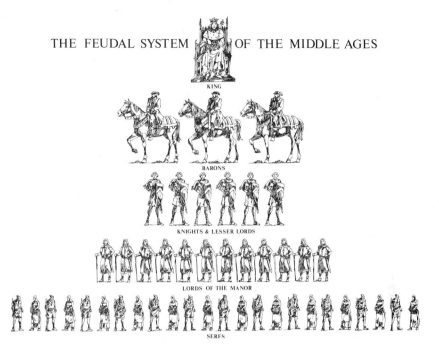

THE FEUDAL SYSTEM OF THE MIDDLE AGES

KING

BARONS

KNIGHTS & LESSER LORDS

LORDS OF THE MANOR

SERFS

The pyramidal arrangement of the feudal system of the Middle Ages is most clearly shown in this diagram.

to the serfs at the bottom who were the food producers. The power of families rose and fell, but the hierarchy remained more or less fixed. Even the decay of feudalism and the decline of serfdom had little impact on a social and political order in which land remained the basis of power, and the local authority of barons or 'magnates' was more important than the king's.

The Catholic Church was also integrated into the social system, and in fact became the greatest of all European landowners. Whereas political power was widely dispersed, the authority of the Church, led by the Pope, was universal, and was never successfully challenged for very long. Catholic doctrine was enforced throughout western and central Europe, and the Church acted as the guardian of literacy and culture, which were mainly expressed in Latin, the universal language of educated people.

The Middle Ages are sometimes called 'the Age of Faith'. However, it would be unwise to suppose that medieval people were less sinful or more pious than Renaissance men and women, who lived through great religious events such as the Protestant Reformation and the

7

The cult of chivalry was a code of behaviour which influenced all aspects of life among the upper classes during Medieval times.

subsequent Catholic revival. But it would be true to say that medieval *attitudes*, the ways in which people thought and felt, were based on their religious beliefs. Among the upper classes, however, attitudes were modified by ideas of chivalry, a cult that some people considered to constitute an alternative religion. Experiences and activities that did not fit into categories of religion or chivalry tended to be ignored or glossed over.

Merchants gained a new importance during the Renaissance, when commerce took over from agriculture as the basis of the economy.

Both religion and chivalry required their followers to observe a code of behaviour rather than to fulfil themselves as individuals. For the rest, as Burckhardt remarks, 'Man was conscious of himself only as a member of a race, people, party, family, or corporation—only through some general category'.

To us, one of the most surprising aspects of the Middle Ages is the lack of interest shown in the distinctive features of the human personality, such as appearance, tricks of speech, gestures, and so on. Medieval writers were at best sketchy in their descriptions of people, and medieval artists generally painted a quality, such as saintliness, rather than an individual.

A changing world

The difference between medieval and modern outlooks became very evident during the Renaissance period. Vital changes were brought about by the growth of towns and trade, which created a society based

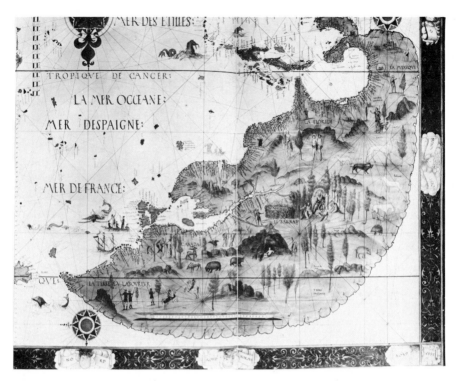

Discoveries of new lands altered the European world view. This is a detail of a map of the world made for Henri II of France.

more on money than on self-sufficient cultivation of the land. Bankers, merchants and traders assumed a new importance and, although still influenced by many of the old values, some developed a distinctive outlook and patronized new types of arts, crafts and literature. Strong, centralized, nation-states such as France, England and Spain emerged and became increasingly powerful. Vernacular literatures (that is, written in the native tongue, not Latin) flourished and began to acquire prestige. The unity of the Church was destroyed by the Protestant Reformation, which eventually provoked a Catholic Counter-Reformation. Both of these were different in important respects from the medieval Church. Printing and gunpowder transformed communications and warfare, while the great voyages, especially Columbus's discovery of the New World, transformed the European conception of the size and scope of the entire world.

As important as any of these was a new attitude to the human personality and the study of human affairs. This, like so many things, made its first appearance in the glittering culture of Renaissance Italy.

2 THE RENAISSANCE IN ITALY

The Italian city-state

In Renaissance Italy, the connections between the new outlook and the growth of towns and trade is clear. By the early fourteenth century, the size and wealth of Florence, Venice, Milan and Naples were greater than those of any city north of the Alps, with the possible exception of Paris. Situated on the trade routes linking northern Europe with the East, the Italian cities prospered and developed sophisticated financial services, including banking, credit arrangements, a reliable currency, and also an information network that existed nowhere else in Europe. Merchants and bankers were proud of their cities and spent lavishly on them. They employed outstanding scholars and writers as civil servants and commissioned painters, sculptors and architects to adorn public and private places. One Florentine writer was moved to ask 'What city ... in all the world is more securely placed within its circle of walls, more proud of its palazzi [palatial houses], more bedecked with churches, more beautiful in its architecture, more imposing in its gates, richer in piazzas [squares], happier in its wide streets, greater in its people, more glorious in its citizenry, more inexhaustible in wealth; more fertile in its fields?'

Florence was the most distinguished of all the Renaissance cities, producing such geniuses as Petrarch in the fourteenth century and Leonardo da Vinci and Michelangelo in the sixteenth century. Although a republic, it came increasingly under the control of a single family, the Medici, who were also the greatest bankers in Europe. In Renaissance Italy, wealth was more important than birth in determining a person's place in the world. But other paths to power and influence also existed. While European warfare was still dominated by the high-born knight, Italians employed professional soldiers, *condottieri*, who fought for pay. If he was clever and lucky, a *condottiere* could become famous and perhaps end his days as the ruler of a state. The most successful of them all, Francesco Sforza, made himself Duke of Milan and founded a dynasty. Pope Pius II, perhaps exaggerating a little, noted that 'In our change-loving Italy where nothing stands firm and no ancient dynasty exists, a servant can easily become a king'.

One reason for this instability was that Italy was divided into many states, which were constantly fighting or combining against one

11

another. Even the largest were dominated by a single city, and are therefore usually known as city-states. Historically the most important were Florence, Venice, Milan, Naples and the Papal States, which were the central Italian states ruled from Rome by the Pope. But many

The Baptistery of St Giovanni in Florence predates the Renaissance, but was a forerunner of the Renaissance style of architecture.

St Croce Church in Florence provides a fine example of Renaissance architecture, and is notable for its frescoes, including some by Giotto.

smaller states such as Urbino, Mantua and Genoa had their moments of glory. Italy's many states provided rich pickings for the *condottieri* and weakened the peninsula against foreign aggressors; but they also made for a dynamic, competitive society. The sheer number of wealthy courts and cities offered wonderful opportunities for patronage to the writers, scholars and artists of the Italian Renaissance.

The 'new learning'

Scholars and artists realized that they were living in new and exciting times, but their way of expressing this fact seems surprising to us. In 1492 the philosopher Marsilio Ficino wrote, 'This century, like a golden age, has restored to light the liberal arts, which were almost extinct: grammar, poetry, rhetoric, painting, sculpture, architecture, music, the ancient singing of songs to the Orphic lyre; and all this in Florence'. The Florentines were, he added, 'Achieving what had

13

Leonardo da Vinci's Mona Lisa *is one of the most famous examples of Renaissance painting.*

A portrait by Botticelli, probably of a member of the Medici family who took control of Florence during the Renaissance.

been honoured among the ancients but almost forgotten since'. Ficino's emphasis is not on creating something new, but on restoring an old, neglected greatness.

That is why we speak of a Renaissance, or rebirth, rather than a new 'birth'. Italians thought of themselves as bringing the splendid culture of ancient Greece and Rome, 'Classical Antiquity', back to life after centuries of supposed medieval darkness. Awareness of the

The paintings on the ceiling of the Sistine Chapel in the Vatican took Michelangelo five years to complete.

Classical past had long existed in Europe, and a good deal of Greek and Roman writing, especially poetry, philosophy and science, was known in the Middle Ages. This awareness had always been especially strong among Italians, who lived in the heartland of the Roman Empire, among the ruins of its mighty buildings and engineering works. From the thirteenth century onwards, a cult of Classical Antiquity grew up in Italy. Dedicated scholars recovered thousands of ancient manuscripts and greatly enlarged European knowledge of the past. Efforts were made to preserve ancient buildings such as the Colosseum in Rome, which had previously been carelessly plundered to provide cheap building materials. Scholarship passed into direct imitation as people strove to live like some chosen classical hero, or to write 'classic' Latin prose modelled on that of Cicero, who lived in the first century BC. The almost superstitious veneration felt for the Greco-Roman achievement is shown in a story which Petrarch, the fourteenth century poet and scholar, told about himself. When a bulky volume toppled from his bookshelves and injured his ankle, he asked himself what he could possibly have done to anger its author, the great Cicero!

However, 'the new learning' of the Renaissance had consequences that went far beyond scholarly discovery or slavish imitation. It bred generations of scholar-writers whom we should now call intellectuals—men who could serve as tutors, archivists, pamphleteers, diplomats or ministers. We actually call them *humanists*, and this word provides the key to the Italian Renaissance. In the letters, histories, dramas, philosophies and other works of Antiquity, the people of the Renaissance found an account of human life and a sense of human greatness that hardly existed in the narrower consciousness of the Middle Ages. They modelled their lives on their knowledge of Antiquity, and lived in a new way. Their interest for us lies in the fact that the people of the Renaissance went far beyond their models, and created one of the world's great historic cultures.

Although Renaissance men and women admired pagan Antiquity, most of them continued to be believing Christians although some, like the youthful philosopher Pico della Mirandola, got into trouble by trying to reconcile the two religions. But the Renaissance outlook was much more human-centred than the medieval view of the world. It placed a new value on the human personality and the potentialities of human beings. Where a medieval author would have stressed the awful responsibility imposed on a human being who had been given the capacity to choose between good and evil, Pico exults: 'O highest

An interest in Classical Antiquity evolved during the Renaissance, saving the Colosseum from being dismantled for building materials.

and marvellous felicity of man! To him it is granted to have whatever he chooses—to be whatever he wills!'

As Pico's emphasis on choice and will suggests, Renaissance man placed a high value on self-development for its own sake—a notion quite unfamiliar to medieval man. The new ideal was the 'universal man' who had mastered a wide range of physical, intellectual and artistic skills. The most versatile of all was Leon Battista Alberti, now chiefly remembered as an architect. He was an expert horseman, soldier, musician, writer, painter and athlete. He could climb mountains and, with his feet together, could jump over the shoulder of a man standing nearby. 'He could endure pain and cold and heat ... showing by example that men can do anything with themselves if they will'—a characteristic Renaissance conclusion.

Alberti and his fellow-Italians were the first men since ancient times to think of life as an art, or rather a set of arts, to be analysed and

Leon Battista Alberti was a prime example of the new 'universal' man of the Renaissance.

A contemporary terra cotta bust of Niccolò Machiavelli, the political philosopher and author of The Prince.

mastered. It was possible to talk of an art of war or an art of love during the Middle Ages; but there was, for example, no art of politics until the Florentine, Niccolò Machiavelli, analysed how men actually behaved (as opposed to the moral fashion in which they *should* have behaved). His book *The Prince* was the first do-it-yourself book for powerseekers. The Renaissance was the first great age of do-it-yourself texts, and one of the most popular handbooks of the time was Baldassare Castiglione's *The Courtier*. This taught all the arts needed for succeeding in high society, from handling a fork properly to telling a good joke.

The invention of printing carried humanist ideas all over Europe, and by the sixteenth century other countries were producing their own

A contemporary painting of Sir Thomas More with his family.

humanists—men such as Thomas More in England and the great Dutch writer Erasmus. The revolution in Italian art also became known. Here, too, the keynote was a new emphasis on humanity. Most medieval art was religious, and the medieval painter in particular tended to stress the awe-inspiring remoteness of religious events. He often emphasized their more-than-human quality by, for example, making figures apparently weightless and even showing them in a variety of sizes, according to their importance rather than their appearance. Renaissance art, although still strongly religious, stressed the human drama and emotions involved in events. This meant that art became 'realistic' in representing people, places and events. This was primarily the achievement of Giotto (c. 1266–1337), whose work was consolidated by the painter Masaccio (1401–28) and the sculptor Donatello (c. 1386–1466). However, the Renaissance interest in the human world greatly widened the scope of art, as demonstrated by developments such as perspective, lifelike portraiture and nude studies. And for the first time since Antiquity, art came to be seen as worth contemplating for its own sake, without reference to some religious or other outside purpose. Not the least of Italian Renaissance achievements was to create the modern conception of what art is about.

The work of the Florentine Donatello reflects the influence of Classical sculpture and contemporary humanist theories.

3 EUROPEAN POWER-STRUGGLES

The sixteenth century is often seen as an age of New Monarchies—strong, centralized states, most of which drew additional strength from their sense of nationhood. Local loyalties began to be replaced by loyalty to the sovereign, and multiple allegiance became less common. (In these, which frequently occurred in the Middle Ages, a man might be a duke in one country, owing allegiance to its sovereign, while simultaneously having a lordship, and therefore obligations, in another state.)

The New Monarchies

The successful New Monarchy developed effective administrative machinery. It controlled the nobility and disarmed 'overmighty subjects'. It evolved a tax system that brought in enough money to give the sovereign freedom of action. Generally speaking, strong monarchs managed to suppress the parliaments and other institutions that had given 'the people' (mainly the better-off) some sort of voice in affairs. And the independent power of the only other competing authority, the Church, was ended, either by a break with the Papacy (such as that of King Henry VIII of England) or by an agreement, such as the Concordat of 1516 which gave King Francis I of France a large measure of control over the French Church. The New Monarch, while not exactly a dictator, exercised far wider powers than most earlier rulers, as lawyers increasingly recognized by quoting maxims such as 'the King's command has the force of law'.

The most internationally active New Monarchies were England, France and Spain. Portugal, preoccupied with expansion overseas, played no significant part in European affairs until the Spanish King Philip II became King of Portugal in 1580. England and France had in fact begun to emerge as nation-states, with distinct identities, during the Middle Ages. But the process was a gradual one, and was completed at a surprisingly late date. (Brittany, for example, became part of France only in 1491.) During the first half of the sixteenth century the most flamboyant monarchs in Europe were Francis I of France and Henry VIII of England. Both were handsome (though his portraits demonstrate why Francis was nicknamed *Roi Grand Nez*, 'King Big Nose'), self-consciously ostentatious and commanding figures. Both

A cartoon showing King Henry VIII of England humiliating the Pope after the Act of Supremacy made him head of the English Church.

were patrons of the arts, who ruled autocratically and, at the slightest provocation, struck cruelly.

As sovereign of a much smaller and less wealthy state, Henry largely wasted his resources by taking part in European wars. Francis' real rival in Europe was the sober Charles I of Spain, better known as the Emperor Charles V. Spain was a *very* 'new' monarchy. The marriage of Isabella of Castille and Ferdinand of Aragon in 1479 created the Spanish state (though the permanence of the union was not assured at the time). The expulsion of the Moors from Granada in 1492 gave

Francis I of France tried to enlist the help of Henry VIII against the Emperor Charles V on the Field of the Cloth of Gold.

them control of the entire peninsula outside Portugal. With Spanish conquests in the New World, wealth flowed into the country, which became the most powerful of sixteenth-century states. For the first half of the century, however, the destiny of Spain was linked with that of an institution that was in no sense a New Monarchy: the Holy Roman Empire.

The Empire
The Holy Roman Empire sprawled right across central Europe, from the Netherlands in the west to Vienna in the east, and the majority of its population were Germans. But its huge size was not an advantage. The Empire was even more divided than Italy, consisting of literally hundreds of self-governing units, including princely territories, bishoprics and cities.

Unlike Italy, the Empire had a ruler. The Holy Roman Emperor had once been the nominal leader of western Christendom, but during the Middle Ages long quarrels with the Popes had crippled the imperial authority. The Papacy had actually encouraged the growth of English and French power as part of its campaign against the emperors. By the sixteenth century, although the Empire had a parliament of sorts

24

(the Diet), the Emperor remained without an effective administration, army or revenue. Princes such as the Elector of Saxony tried to make sure that things stayed that way, since they valued their independence.

The Emperor would have been powerless if he had not been able to back his authority with private resources. Although the emperors were elected, the office was always held from 1438 by a member of the Habsburg family. The Habsburgs possessed lands in various parts of the Empire, but their main strength lay in their Austrian duchies in the south east. These enabled Habsburg emperors to hold their own with the German princes, although they were unable to dominate them.

The Habsburgs were not particularly distinguished as rulers, but they had a knack of making useful marriage alliances which increased their territorial holdings. *Bella gerant alii, tu, felix Austria, nube* became a well-known saying: 'let others make war, you, happy Austria, marry'. The greatest of all Habsburg coups occurred when the young Charles von Habsburg inherited in quick succession Burgundy (which included the Netherlands—modern Belgium and Holland), Austria and Spain.

The shaded areas of this map show the extent of the Habsburg Empire in Europe in the early sixteenth century.

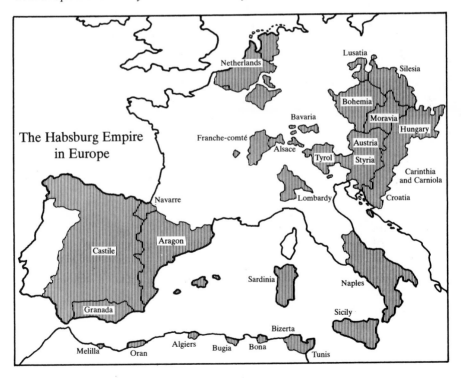

25

King Charles I of Spain became Emperor Charles V of the Habsburg Empire and was later elected Emperor of the Holy Roman Empire.

This tapestry depicts the Battle of Pavia in which Charles V was victorious over Francis I.

Then, still only nineteen, he was elected Holy Roman Emperor as Charles V in 1519.

The struggle for dominion

This dramatically changed the situation in Europe and the Empire. Charles possessed vast territories and also vast resources, in the form of taxes from the Netherlands. The towns of the Low Countries had grown immensely wealthy through trade and manufacturing. Later, Charles was also enriched by silver from the mines of the New World, which were soon producing abundantly for their Spanish masters. Charles' chief adviser, Gattinara, told him 'God ... has raised you above all the kings and princes of Christendom ... He has set you on the path towards a world monarchy'.

Whether the traditionally-minded Charles aimed at such a monarchy is another matter. But the fear of it raised up enemies against him. These included the German princes, who were afraid that Charles might be able to make imperial authority a reality, and above all Francis I, who feared the complete encirclement of his kingdom. For much of Francis's reign the conflict between France and the Empire was fought out mainly in Italy. The French had been pursuing claims to Milan and Naples since 1494, when the invasion by Charles VIII of France set off a long series of Italian wars. The Italian states found themselves reduced to the roles of victims or satellites (dependants) once the great powers had intervened; and this sapped the vitality of the Renaissance. The Franco-Imperial conflict continued throughout

27

An allegorical painting of the Emperor Charles V leading his troops into battle.

the reigns of Charles V and Francis I, but its Italian phase effectively ended in 1529 with the Peace of Cambrai. By then it was clear that Charles had won. He gained control of Milan and Naples, and Florence and Genoa became Habsburg satellites. Only the Papal States and a gradually declining Venice retained any independence; almost all the rest of Italy was to remain under the shadow of the Habsburgs for centuries.

Even with this success, Charles discovered that the unwieldiness of his empire was as significant as its strength. Fighting the French took up much of his energy. When the French were quiet, the Empire was inflamed by the turbulence of the German princes, many of whom had converted to the heretical (Protestant) doctrines of Martin Luther. And when he was not warring with the French or the German princes, Charles had to contend with the Ottoman Turks, who threatened Christendom both in south-east Europe and in the Mediterranean.

Charles held his inheritance together, although he failed to turn the Holy Roman Empire into a workable monarchy. But the effort was finally too much for him. 'Today I feel so exhausted that I could not help you, as you see yourselves. In my present state of dejection and weakness I . . . lay aside my authority.' In 1555 he abdicated, dividing his empire. His brother Ferdinand became Holy Roman Emperor,

King Philip II of Spain championed the Counter-Reformation in Europe.

retaining the traditional Habsburg lands, and Charles's son became the most powerful man in Europe as Philip II, King of Spain and ruler of Spanish America, the Netherlands and Habsburg Italy.

Wars of religion
'Rather than suffer the least hurt to religion and the service of God, I would lose all my realms ... for I neither intend nor desire to be the ruler of heretics,' wrote Philip II. He was perfectly sincere; but his course of action was made simpler by the fact that his leading enemies were Protestants. (Ironically, the main exceptions were the Popes, who as central Italian rulers tended to be unfriendly to the dominant Spanish.) In western Europe, the history of the later sixteenth century is largely a record of heroic Spanish efforts to destroy the Protestant heresy. If this had occurred, England and France would have been reduced to being Spanish satellites. From 1566 a rebellion against Philip's heavy-handed regime in the Netherlands became increasingly identified with the Protestant cause. Protestant England, under Queen Elizabeth I, helped the Dutch rebels, while English seamen raided Spanish colonies and robbed Spanish ships of the American silver that kept Philip's empire going. And in the religious civil wars

On the day before her coronation, Queen Elizabeth I of England was carried in a litter through the crowded streets of London.

The Armada was sent by Philip II of Spain against England in 1588. It was defeated by the navy of Elizabeth I.

that crippled France, Philip backed the Catholic party and Elizabeth the Huguenots (Protestants).

Despite tremendous expense of both blood and treasure, the Spanish effort failed. Defeated at sea or wrecked by the weather, Philip's armadas were never able to mount an invasion of England. The Spanish held on to the southern Netherlands (now Belgium), but failed to reconquer the north (Holland). And in France, the Huguenot leader Henri of Navarre (Henri IV) inherited the throne and shrewdly made himself acceptable to his opponents (especially the fiercely Catholic Parisians) by allowing himself to be converted to Catholicism, remarking cynically that 'Paris is worth a mass'. After this, Henri was able to unite Frenchmen against the Spanish on a national rather than a religious basis.

Over-ambitious policies, economic mismanagement and stifling religious orthodoxy had begun to exhaust Spain by the end of the sixteenth century. In the seventeenth century, Spain was replaced by a newly-united France as the dominant European state, while the Dutch United Provinces and England emerged as great maritime and commercial powers.

4 REFORMATION AND COUNTER-REFORMATION

The Reformation was at least as important as the Renaissance in the making of modern Europe. The revolt against the Catholic Church broke the unity of western Christendom and ushered in more than a century of ferocious religious wars. One paradoxical result was that, because neither the Catholics nor the various Protestant sects were able to achieve victory, religious conflict eventually caused the growth of toleration in a number of countries.

The condition of the Church

During the Middle Ages, the Church had been through periods of corruption and scandal. But it had always succeeded in reforming itself without sacrificing its authority. The fifteenth and early sixteenth

An anti-papal cartoon depicting the burning of the English Protestant bishops Latimer and Ridley, during the reign of the Catholic Queen Mary.

Martin Luther initiated the Protestant Reformation, which was a revolt against the corruptions of the Roman Catholic Church.

Luther nailed his theses to the door of the church at Wittenberg.

century was another period of corruption, most shocking of all, at the very top. A series of Renaissance popes, such as Alexander VI, Julius II and Leo X, were thoroughly worldly figures, ready to buy their way to the Papacy and use its power to glorify themselves and advance their families (which often, despite their priestly vow of celibacy, included their own children). In the world of politics, they were mainly concerned to strengthen their hold on the Papal States in central Italy. They operated just like other rulers, and Pope Julius II even put on armour and led his troops to war. Similar complaints were made about the rest of the clergy—of bishops who neglected their sees, monks and friars who wallowed in riches and idleness, and parish priests who were too ignorant to carry out their duties properly.

Such discontent was potentially dangerous, since the Church occupied a privileged place both in religious and secular matters. It claimed absolute authority in matters of belief, and presented itself as the only mediator between man and God. There was 'no salvation outside the Church'. The priest had a special place in the mass; only he partook of both bread and wine—the body and blood of Christ—while the laity had to be content with the bread. He was also supported by special taxes and answerable for many of his failings only to a special church court with its own rules (canon law). A corrupt Church which failed to reform was therefore likely to find its wider claims challenged. This was especially true in a period when rising national feeling made people resent paying taxes to 'foreigners' like the pope; while strong national rulers were becoming intolerant of rival authorities and casting greedy eyes on the wealth of the Church.

If the Church's authority was shaken, its teaching would be questioned, for example about practices such as the cult of the Virgin and praying to saints, which had grown up over the centuries. These might be justifiable if, as Catholics believed, the traditions of the Church were as valid as the Scriptures. If they were not—and a corrupt Church made it easy to think so—an attempt would have to be made to return to the practice of the early, uncorrupted Church. Even before the Reformation, there were many people—especially lay men and women—who were trying to achieve a simpler, more inward religious life in which they experienced direct contact with God. This tendency, combined with nationalism, princely power and other factors, produced a mighty revolt against the Church. It was set off by one man, Martin Luther.

The reformers

Luther, a miner's son, was a scholar-monk who had become Professor of Theology at the University of Wittenberg. He became nationally famous in 1517, when he challenged the system of indulgences. These were certificates, sold by the Church authorities, that supposedly freed the buyer from sin and guilt, or did the same for the souls of the dead in purgatory. In Catholicism, purgatory was the place or state where sins were atoned for before the soul was allowed into heaven. One of the more flamboyant salesmen of indulgences was the Dominican monk Johannes Tetzel. He assured simple folk that 'as the coin rattles in my box, the soul flies up to heaven'!

When Tetzel's activities brought him close to Wittenberg, Luther protested. He nailed ninety-five theses onto the door of the University church. These were propositions which he was prepared to defend in the fashion that was traditional in universities. The matter might have remained a scholarly issue, but the Church authorities reacted harshly and the recent invention of printing gave the controversy wide publicity. German public opinion buoyed up Luther's cause, and he reinforced its effect through writing, such as the famous *Address to the Christian Nobility of Germany* of 1520.

Luther was condemned by the Pope, and in 1521 he was summoned to face the Diet of the Holy Roman Empire, presided over by the Emperor Charles V. When called on to withdraw his opinions, he made a typical declaration: 'Unless I am proved wrong by Scripture or by reasoning—I do not accept the decisions of Councils or Popes, for they err and contradict one another—my conscience is captive to the word of God . . . I cannot and will not recant anything'. In denying the authority of the Church, appealing to the Scriptures, and relying on private judgement or conscience, this statement conveys some of the most important aspects of Protestantism.

Inevitably, once Protestantism became a separate force, it developed further away from Catholicism, differing from it on many points. It also produced new interpreters—the Swiss Zwingli at Zurich in the 1520s, and above all Jean Calvin at Geneva in the next generation. Whereas much of Luther's teaching remained traditional, Calvin was more radical. He dispensed with bishops and archbishops, and made Geneva a model city in which clergy and laity collaborated in enforcing 'godly' behaviour. Most people would now find the Calvinist system oppressive, but the Scottish reformer John Knox hailed it as 'the most perfect school of Christ that ever was on earth since the days of the apostles'. This 'school' trained generations of religious radicals from other countries, making Calvinism a great international movement.

Action and reaction

Lutheranism divided the Holy Roman Empire, leading to religious wars that lasted until 1555, when a compromise peace was made. Lutheranism had thrived with the support of powerful German princes, and this was also true of the Scandinavian kingdoms and England.

*Johannes Tetzel was a German Dominican monk, whose selling of
indulgences provoked Luther's ninety-five theses at Wittenberg.*

Jean Calvin led the Protestant Reformation in France and Switzerland, and was particularly admired by the Scottish reformer, John Knox.

John Knox established the Presbyterian Church of Scotland, after returning from exile in 1560.

In all these states, sincerity was mixed up with princely self-interest, which benefited from control of the Church and its wealth. But the 'reformed religion' also made progress in Poland, Bohemia, the Netherlands, Scotland and France. By the 1540s it may well have seemed that Catholicism was collapsing.

However, Catholicism proved capable of self-renewal. The Counter-Reformation, or Catholic Reformation, created a militant faith that succeeded in checking the spread of Protestantism. From the time of Pope Paul III, the popes were men of some energy and conviction, although family and political interests still influenced their actions. A general council of the Church, the Council of Trent, met intermittently from 1545 and defined Catholic doctrine in such a way that there was no possibility of a compromise with heresy. Religious enthusiasm was channeled into new associations of laymen and priests, and new orders were founded, above all the Society of Jesus, created by the Spaniard

Ignatius Loyola founded the Society of Jesus in 1534.

St Ignatius Loyola. Its members, the Jesuits, owed complete obedience to the Pope and served as the 'shock-troops of the Counter-Reformation'. They transformed Catholic education, served as missionaries to heretic and heathen alike, and exercised much behind-the-scenes influence as the confessors and advisers of kings. In Catholic Europe, freedom of thought was repressed even more completely than in Protestant lands, through institutions such as the Inquisition and the Index (an official list of forbidden reading).

Between them, the Reformation and the Counter-Reformation broke with the medieval past and divided Europe into two very different types of society.

5 THE ART OF WAR

Two changes made sixteenth-century warfare quite distinct from everything that had occurred during the Middle Ages. On land the heavy-armed knight on horseback became obsolete, and at sea the sailing ship became the dominant fighting machine.

Fire-power supreme

In the fifteenth century the armoured and mounted man was still an important figure in most armies, although he had lost the total supremacy he had once enjoyed. The use of longbows, early guns, and pikes all modified battle tactics considerably and, around 1500, the most successful of these were pikes. Organized in close columns like bristling hedgehogs, well-disciplined pikemen could move at speed and achieve a tank-like impact. The finest of all were the Swiss, who hired themselves out to the highest bidder and won most of their battles without very much help from either cavalry or artillery.

In the fifteenth century gunpowder had been a useful but unreliable aid in battle. Improvements in the sixteenth century made firearms a decisive factor in war. At Marignano in 1515, artillery and cavalry swung the battle against the Swiss defenders of Milan and gave Francis I his most famous victory. But it was the Spanish victory at Bicocca in 1522 that broke the Swiss pikemen, who were mown down by a new weapon, the arquebus. This was the first light, reasonably accurate gun, resembling a rifle. Thanks to the invention of the matchlock, it fired when a trigger was pulled instead of needing to be ignited while somebody else held it steady. The Spanish arquebusiers' greatest triumph was at the battle of Pavia in 1525. Under concentrated fire, the French pikemen broke and ran, while the flower of French knighthood charged again and again, only to be picked off by the arquebusiers concealed in trees and bushes. Francis himself became Charles V's prisoner, and the completeness of the disaster is conveyed in the letter he wrote to his mother. It began, 'To let you know the extent of my misfortune, nothing remains to me except my honour and my life'.

The supremacy of fire-power was emphasized by the introduction of the wheel-lock pistol at the battle of Mühlberg in 1547, where Charles V crushed his Protestant foes among the German princes. Like Pavia, it seemed to promise a great extension of the Emperor's power, but in the event only raised up new enemies against him. By this time the knight with the lance had virtually disappeared, and armies

As the use of gunpowder became more refined, arquebusiers played an increasingly important role in sixteenth-century battle tactics.

Siege warfare became the order of the day during the sixteenth century, as the firing range of firearms increased.

consisted of arquebusiers backed up by pikemen and light cavalry armed with javelins and pistols. Towards the end of the century the arquebus was supplemented by the musket, a heavy handgun which had to be supported on a forked rest but which was more accurate and longer-ranged.

The effectiveness of guns at a distance gave the defending side a great advantage. Because of this, in the later sixteenth century, all-or-nothing pitched battles were quite rare. Siege warfare became the order of the day, especially in the Netherlands, where the difficult, river-crossed terrain turned the conflict between the Dutch and Spanish into a war of attrition. Throughout the sixteenth century, the Spanish troops were the finest in Christian Europe. The great Spanish commanders such as Parma and Spinola would probably have reconquered the Netherlands if they had not been distracted by other calls on their resources. Parma in particular had been steadily advancing against the Dutch until he was forced to intervene on Philip II's orders in the French Wars of Religion.

The age of fighting sail
The revolution in naval warfare was even more thoroughgoing. In the late Middle Ages, new techniques and instruments allowed seamen

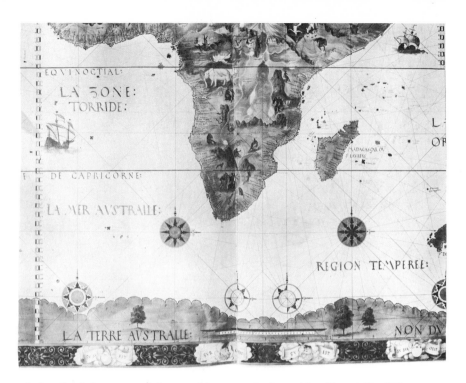

A detail of the map of the world, commissioned by Henri II of France, showing the Cape of Good Hope.

to take their ships into the open sea instead of hugging the coastlines. The Portuguese eventually sailed round the Cape of Good Hope into the Indian Ocean, while the Spaniards crossed the Atlantic to the New World. Their small, square-rigged, three-masted ships, armed with cannon, possessed a manoeuvrability and fire-power that made them almost unbeatable wherever they went.

In the sixteenth century, Europeans began to exploit these advantages in the wars they fought with one another. Previously they had used galleys, which were mainly propelled by oars and used in landlubberly fashion to board the enemy and overcome him in hand-to-hand fighting. Perhaps because she was surrounded by sea, England took an early lead in developing a new type of ocean-going warship, the galleon. The tall, clumsy gun-castles, which commanded the enemy's decks, were dispensed with. Instead, the cargo deck was lined with cannon, enabling galleons to deliver devastating 'broadsides'. A combination of superior technology and seamanship gave the English a tremendous advantage in the undeclared war with Spain during the

1570s, when Francis Drake and others plundered Spanish colonies and held up Spanish treasure-ships. The Spaniards, accustomed to fighting with galleys in the Mediterranean, learned more slowly. But after Philip II of Spain also became King of Portugal, they began to assemble a formidable fleet of galleons. The conflict between the English seadogs and the Spanish Armada in 1588 was the first of its kind, and full of errors and misjudgements. (Both sides ran out of ammunition, although the English, being closer to home, found it easier to re-supply.) English seamanship won the day, but it was bad weather that turned the Armada's flight into a disaster. The defeat of the Armada ended the immediate threat of invasion, but in later years the Spanish navy was greatly improved, and there was a long and dour struggle before the two countries made peace in 1604.

Galleons, such as this one belonging to Henry VIII of England, could deliver devastating 'broadsides' to enemy vessels.

The Turkish threat

On the other side of Europe, quarrels between the states of Christian Europe had made it easy for the Ottoman Turks to advance in the Balkans and the Mediterranean. In 1526, under Sultan Suleiman the Magnificent, the Turks captured Belgrade and smashed the Hungarian army at the battle of Mohacs. Most of Hungary then passed under Turkish control, and for a time in 1529 they even besieged Habsburg Vienna. However, much of the Turkish effort in the sixteenth century took the form of naval and military advances in the Mediterranean. By capturing Rhodes in 1522 and greatly weakening the maritime power of Venice, the Turks became the dominant power in the Mediterranean.

Francis Drake was a great nuisance to the Spanish, and instrumental in the defeat of the Armada in 1588.

Old-fashioned galleys like these were used in the Battle of Lepanto, which brought the Turkish threat to an end.

But their advance brought them up against the growing power of Spain. In 1565 the Knights of St John managed to survive the long and savage siege of Malta until relieved by a Spanish force. Then in 1571 the crucial battle took place off the coast of Greece at Lepanto. This battle was old-fashioned in that it was fought between fleets of galleys. But it was notable for the size of the fleets (there were 200 to 300 ships on each side) and the ferocity with which the battle between rival faiths was fought. The Christian fleet, consisting of Spanish, Venetian and Papal ships and commanded by Don John of Austria, half-brother to Philip II, won an overwhelming victory whose fame echoed round contemporary Europe. The bells were rung even in Protestant London to celebrate 'the overthrow of the Turk'.

Lepanto was not a decisive defeat for the Turks, but it proved to be a turning point. Psychologically its effect was immense. The Spanish novelist Cervantes described it in *Don Quixote* as 'that day, so fortunate for Christendom, when all nations were undeceived of their error in believing that the Turks were invincible'. And during the breathing-space provided by the victory, the Turkish empire began to lose its forward impetus, falling into gradual decline from the seventeenth century onwards.

6 LITERATURE AND THE ARTS

By 1500, the art and culture of Renaissance Italy already had a long history, though they had still not made their full impact on the rest of Europe.

The visual arts

Although many Italian cities contributed to the Renaissance, Florence was easily the most important until about 1500. Her place was then taken by Rome, where the Popes became art patrons on a grand scale. The early sixteenth century is often labelled 'The High Renaissance', since it produced three supreme geniuses—Leonardo da Vinci, Michelangelo and Raphael. Their contemporaries were most impressed with

A painting by Raphael who was a product of the 'High Renaissance' and is regarded as one of its greatest artists.

Michelangelo was a painter, sculptor and architect. This famous sculpture, La Pieta, *is housed in St Peter's, Rome.*

The Flemish painter Pieter Breughel incorporated both vigour and great emotional content into his paintings.

'the divine Michelangelo', a sculptor and painter of heroic energy whose Sistine Chapel paintings alone would be enough to make him one of the greatest artists of all time. The medieval artist had often been anonymous but the Renaissance artist was admired and sought-after. With Michelangelo, the artist became a special kind of being for the first time—a genius who was respected for his creative talents alone.

Outside Italy, the outstanding school of painting was in the Netherlands. Masters such as Jan van Eyck developed their own meticulously realistic style although they were certainly influenced by Italian art. The native tradition remained strong in the sixteenth century, ranging from the earthy vigour of Pieter Breughel the elder to the obscure and bizarre religious symbolism of Hieronymous Bosch. Like many northerners, Albrecht Dürer, who was German, studied in Italy. He absorbed the Renaissance style, although he brought to it the sombre and inward-looking quality which was characteristic of many north Europeans. Francis I imported Italian painters as palace decorators, and sheltered Leonardo da Vinci during the artist's last years. Even far-away England employed Italian artists, until the Reformation cut her off from the Catholic world; the German portrait painter Hans Holbein was a source of new ideas, and his main English follower was Nicholas Hilliard, a painter of exquisite miniatures.

Meanwhile, in Italy, the Renaissance was petering out. Its end is often said to be the year 1527, when Charles V's mutinous soldiers sacked Rome with great brutality. It is certainly true that this disaster shocked the Papacy and helped to create the more serious, intense

A painting by Albrecht Durer who was regarded as the greatest German Renaissance artist.

The English artist Nicholas Hilliard painted many exquisite, intricately detailed miniatures.

and exalted atmosphere associated with the Counter-Reformation. The classic calm of Renaissance art gave way to the agitated Mannerist and Baroque styles, which are reflected in the later work of Michelangelo. Caravaggio, an Italian painter, and El Greco, a 'Spanish' painter born in Crete, ushered in a new art of movement, drama and high emotion which dominated the seventeenth century. Only in sixteenth-century Venice did the Renaissance persist a little longer, through remarkable colourists such as Titian and Veronese. Titian was long-lived and enormously productive, and one of his outstanding gifts was as a portrait painter. He could create people who strike us as being distinct individuals—a Renaissance trait that also appears again and again in sixteenth-century writing.

A painting by El Greco in the tradition of the 'Spanish' school.

Literature

Despite their achievements in education, scholarship, Biblical investigation and other fields, the Renaissance humanists are not widely read today. This is partly because they wrote in Latin—already a 'dead'

Desiderius Erasmus was a noted Dutch humanist and satirical writer.

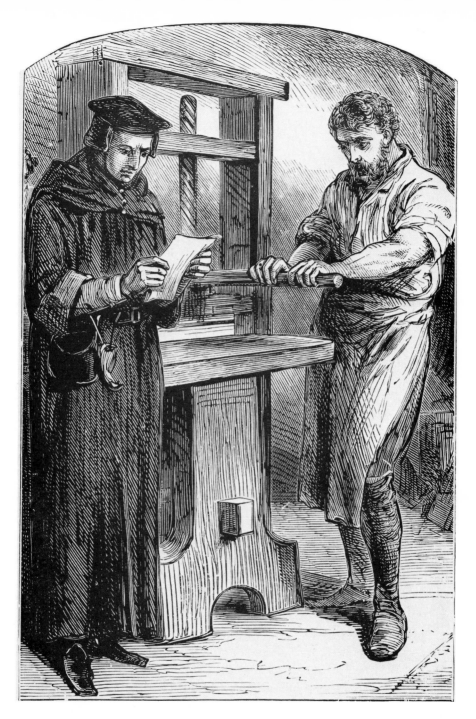

This nineteenth-century picture of William Caxton shows him reading proofs from the printing press which he introduced to England in 1477.

language—and partly because they modelled themselves too closely on ancient Roman authors to succeed in creating original literature. The main exception was the Dutchman Erasmus, a scholar and wit whose merciless mockery of clerical abuses helped to bring on the Reformation crisis, although he himself remained within the Catholic Church. His English friend, Thomas More, was a man of similar principles, who was executed for opposing Henry VIII's religious changes. More's *Utopia* gave a new word to the language and was the first description of an imaginary 'ideal' society.

The future belonged to the vernacular languages. In the sixteenth century books, poems and plays appeared in huge quantities, stimulated by the Renaissance, the Reformation and the new invention of printing. Machiavelli's *Prince*, Castiglione's *Courtier* and other 'do-it-yourself' books were written in Italian. Luther wrote in Latin as a scholar and in German as a passionate controversialist. His translation of the Bible has been called the beginning of German literature. Vernacular Bibles, replacing the Latin version in Protestant countries, were a major achievement of the Reformation. In England, Tyndale and others produced translations that were finally incorporated in the great Authorized ('King James') Version of 1611.

The Renaissance interest in personalities was reflected in the publication of the earliest autobiographies that were not mainly concerned with the subject's religious life. Benvenuto Cellini wrote a racy account of his doings in Italian, since 'everyone who has to his credit . . . great achievements . . . ought to write the story of his own life'. The French magistrate Michel de Montaigne conducted a more scrupulous self-examination in a new literary form, the essay. Biographies also became common, and the publication of Giorgio Vasari's *Lives of the Artists* indicated the new status of painters, sculptors and architects.

The sixteenth century was also a great age of epic poetry. Much of it was concerned with love and chivalry, but Camoes' *Lusiads* struck a more 'modern' note, describing the heroic overseas adventures of the Portuguese. By contrast, Rabelais stretched the resources of the French language to its limits in his fantastic *Gargantua and Pantagruel*. An anonymous Spaniard invented a form of low-life (picaresque) novel in *Lazarillo de Tormes*. The exalted tone of Spanish life was mocked by Cervantes in his great anti-chivalric novel *Don Quixote*.

As with the visual arts, forms and ideas were imported and adapted from Renaissance Italy. This was particularly true of Tudor England, where the sonnet and other poetic forms were anglicized, and many

Right   *Miles Coverdale was the first to translate the Bible into English. His version was published in 1535.*

56

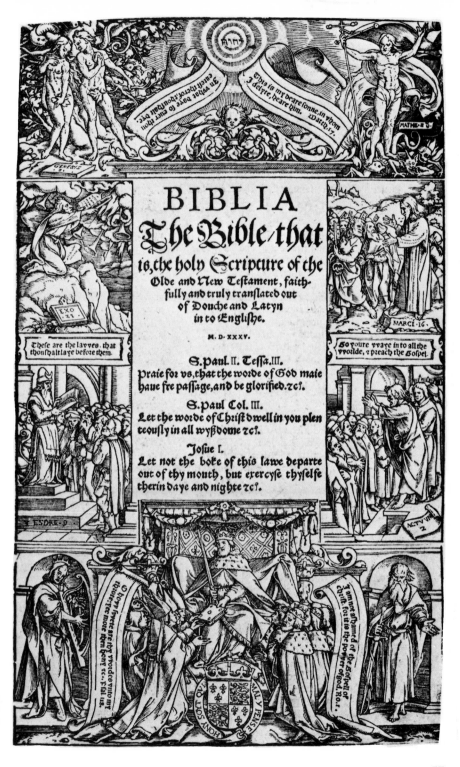

BIBLIA

The Bible, that

is, the holy Scripture of the
Olde and New Testament, faith-
fully and truly translated out
of Douche and Latyn
in to Englishe.

M. D. XXXV.

S. paul. II. Tessa. III.
Praie for vs, that the worde of God maie
haue fre passage, and be glorified. zc̄.

S. paul Col. III.
Let the worde of Christ dwell in you plen
teously in all wyßdome zc̄.

Josue I.
Let not the boke of this lawe departe
out of thy mouth, but exercyse thyselfe
therin daye and nighte zc̄.

of the finest works produced were translations. The result of so much borrowing was a literature of astonishing quality and range. This is shown in such works as Spenser's *Faerie Queene*, the pamphlets of Robert Greene, and the dramas of Shakespeare.

William Shakespeare is thought by many to be the greatest poet and dramatist that England has ever produced.

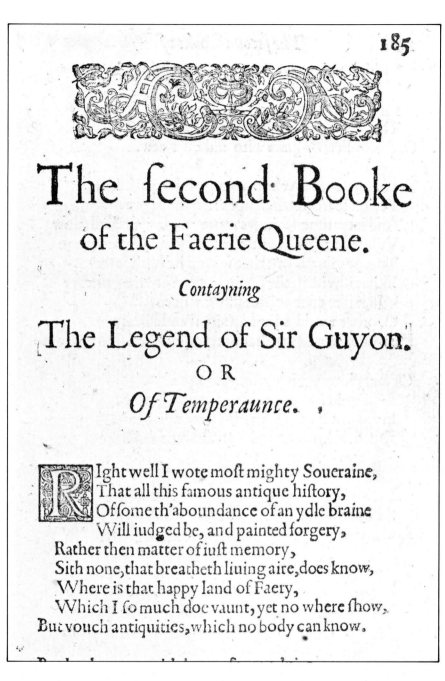

The second Booke
of the Faerie Queene.

Contayning

The Legend of Sir Guyon.
O R
Of Temperaunce.

Ight well I wote moſt mighty Soueraine,
That all this famous antique hiſtory,
Of ſome th'aboundance of an ydle braine
Will iudged be, and painted forgery,
Rather then matter of iuſt memory,
Sith none, that breatheth liuing aire, does know,
Where is that happy land of Faery,
Which I ſo much doe vaunt, yet no where ſhow,
But vouch antiquities, which no body can know.

Edmund Spenser was an English poet. He was celebrated for his work
The Faerie Queene *which was an allegorical romance. It was*
illustrative of the quality of late Renaissance literature.

Music

In music, the composers and performers of the Netherlands school had the kind of prestige that the Italians enjoyed in the visual arts. Great composers such as Josquin des Prés and Orlandus de Lassus were revered and imitated. Choirmasters, singers and instrumentalists from the Netherlands worked all over Europe.

During the sixteenth century, Venice and other Italian centres took over the lead from the Netherlands. The most famous Italian composer was Giovanni da Palestrina. His fluent, even-textured church music

The composer Giovanni da Palestrina is shown presenting his Mass *to Pope Julius III.*

This detail from Thoinot Arbeau's Orchesographie *shows musicians playing for a dance.*

was in keeping with the Counter-Reformation rule that music must not distract the worshipper from the word of God.

The Italians also developed the madrigal, which is a song with several separate vocal parts sung together. This became very popular in England, where every educated person was supposed to be able to sing a part. The madrigal's appeal for English people may have been founded in the prominence it gave to the words. But England also produced great composers of instrumental and church music of her own, such as Dowland and Byrd.

At the very end of the sixteenth century a new musical form was created, due to the continued Italian reverence for Antiquity. The *camerata*, a group of musicians and intellectuals in Florence, decided to revive the ancient Greek form of drama. They were convinced that Greek actors had sung their lines, but they were wrong. In composing supposedly Greek dramas, they gave the world the opera. This quickly became the vehicle for great art, as in *Orfeo* (1607) and other works by Claudio Monteverdi.

7 SOCIAL AND ECONOMIC LIFE

Despite changes in the arts, war and religion, the traditional order in Europe remained largely intact. Kings tended to be more powerful than before, but they still ruled over nobles with great territorial possessions, and the upper classes kept up the fiction that they were a knightly order, taking part in spectacular and dangerous tournaments. Rank continued to be maintained, marriages to be arranged, children to be flogged. Superstition remained widespread; the sixteenth and seventeenth centuries produced their own examples in the witch-hunting mania that claimed thousands of victims. Apart from printing, arms manufacturing and navigational instruments, there were few technological advances to disrupt the traditional way of life. Most people still

Superstition was widespread during the Renaissance. This picture from the Cosmographie Universelle *shows a gypsy telling fortunes.*

The traditional way of life was not disrupted during the Renaissance; most people were still farmers living in small villages.

worked on the land (though few of them were now serfs), and lived in villages or smaller settlements.

Merchants, towns and trade

Nevertheless, new economic activity was bringing about great changes. Unlike his medieval predecessor, the sixteenth-century farmer did not aim to be self-sufficient, satisfying only his own needs, but produced goods for the market, which earned him cash. His surpluses helped to feed the towns growing up in most parts of Europe, and his ability to buy goods stimulated trade and the growth of a money economy. This was not an age of manufacturing (with a few exceptions such as cloth and shipbuilding), but of commerce. The wealthy merchant class, though far from dominant, assumed a new importance. The most enterprising became what we should now call financiers, dealing with

Vasco da Gama, who discovered the route around the Cape of Good Hope in 1498, is presented to the King of India.

investments through an international network of contacts. The Fuggers of Augsberg were the greatest sixteenth-century financiers, and they put out their own *Newsletter*. Their loans smoothed Charles V's election to the imperial throne and were partly repaid with titles of nobility. Eventually, however, they over-invested in the Habsburgs, whose bankruptcies crippled the firm. An equally modern-seeming figure was Sir Thomas Gresham, who looked after Queen Elizabeth I of England's interests on the Antwerp money market, where speculation in currencies and commodities was already rife.

The European economy was dramatically affected by the late fifteenth-century discoveries of the New World and the route to India round the Cape of Good Hope. Europe's most important trade was with the East, which provided spices, silks, muslins and pearls. Venice and Genoa had grown rich by purchasing these goods in the ports of the eastern Mediterranean and carrying them back to Italy in their galleys. The towns all along the trade routes through Italy and Germany to the Baltic and Netherlands had prospered as a result of this. Vasco da Gama's discovery of a sea route to India made direct buying possible, cutting out a host of middlemen operating throughout the Middle East. The Portuguese were able to revolutionize trade by selling spices and other goods at a far lower price than the Venetians. The New World seemed less important at first, until quantities of bullion, especially silver, began to be shipped to Europe during the sixteenth century. The result of these events was the slow decline of the Mediterranean and central European lands, and the rise of the countries on the Atlantic sea board. Until this time England had been an underpopulated little country on the edge of the known world, but this development led to a growth in her importance over the next few centuries.

Silver from the New World was at least partly responsible for a new development which was only possible in a money economy —inflation. This is sometimes defined as 'too much money chasing too few goods', resulting in a general rise in prices. Silver poured into Spain, and poured straight out again into Europe to pay for the international ambitions of Charles V and Philip II. Population increase may also have contributed to inflation, since the increased demand for food would also have pushed up prices. This was shown in the fact that the steepest price rises occurred in agricultural produce. Sixteenth-century people knew very little about economics, and generally blamed human wickedness for inflation. The English Bishop Latimer, for example, lamented that, because of landlords' greed, a property 'before

Bishop Hugh Latimer believed that the high rate of inflation in England was due to human greed.

went for twenty or forty pound by year ... now is let for fifty or an hundred pound'. He warned that one of these days a mere pig would not sell for less than a pound.

Inflation hit people whose incomes could not keep up with rising prices. The English monarchy, for example, got into difficulties

Renaissance people enjoyed more comforts at home, such as glass and pewter, and a wider variety of foods, than their predecessors.

People became 'fashion-conscious' for the first time; men sported peascod doublets and padded hose.

under Elizabeth I and her successors because most of its revenues were fixed and traditional. In general, commercially-minded landlords and merchants benefited, while the poorest people, who were least able to resist their landlords or secure higher wages, became worse off. Greater wealth and wider horizons were characteristic of the period, but only for certain sections of the population. Not surprisingly this was also a century of riots and rebellions, often inflamed by religious disputes. The German Peasants' Revolt of 1524–25 was partly inspired by Lutheranism, although Luther himself denounced the revolt. But other movements, such as the Pilgrimage of Grace of 1536 in England, occurred in defence of 'the old religion'. Both were savagely put down. The age, even more than most, favoured the strong and successful.

Fashion and manners
Standards of living rose rapidly for the successful. Their houses were larger and more comfortable. They had glass in the windows, glasses and pewter pots for drinking, plate on the sideboard, four-poster beds, and a wider range of furniture and furnishings.

Food became more plentiful and interesting. Meat retained its prestige as the item for 'conspicuous consumption', but vegetables and fruit were more widely grown and eaten. The New World offered new foods such as tomatoes, drinking chocolate, bananas, avocados and turkey. Even the poor benefited from the arrival in Europe of the potato and maize. More dubious imports were sugar (known but not widely used until cultivated in the West Indies) and tobacco.

Manners, including table manners, were refined under the influence of Italian authors like Castiglione and Della Casa, author of the *Galateo*. Among other things, they insisted that the true gentleman should not eat with his fingers. But even at the end of the century Englishmen looked with suspicion on a new-fangled Italian invention—the fork.

In dress, the sixteenth century can be recognized as the first period in which fashion ruled; that is, in which modes of dress changed rapidly and it became a matter of pride to be up-to-date. The extravagances of the age culminated in the great cartwheel ruff worn by both sexes, the stiff 'peascod belly' doublet and padded hose of the men and the 'walking tent' farthingale skirt worn by women.

A wider world?

Though Europeans were finding their way all over the world, few of them as yet questioned their national and religious prejudices. They went abroad to plunder, to convert, or to 'civilize' rather than to learn in any but a narrowly factual way from their explorations.

Sixteenth-century science made little headway, partly because the humanists' admiration for ancient authorities actually discouraged independent investigation. An important exception was Andrea Vesalius, the first person to study anatomy by dissecting human bodies.

The highly fashionable farthingale skirt was worn by ladies at Court during the Renaissance.

Andrea Vesalius was the father of anatomical research.

His *Fabric of the Human Body* of 1543 was an epoch-making publication which led on to Harvey's discovery of the circulation of the blood early in the next century.

However, educated men began to take notice of the unorthodox views of Copernicus. He held that the earth went round the sun, and not vice versa. His writings, like the observations of Tycho Brahe in Denmark, contradicted the ancient theory of Ptolemy. The Ptolemaic

Nicolaus Copernicus introduced a new theory of the solar system.

theory had been elaborated during the Middle Ages into a complete world-view that made the earth—and humanity—the centre of the universe. The overthrow of the man-centred medieval universe was to be one of the achievements of the next century.

DATE CHART

1492	Columbus discovers America	1558	Elizabeth becomes Queen of England
1494	French invasion begins Italian wars	1559	Peace of Cateau-Cambrésis between France and Spain
1497	Vasco da Gama reaches India via Cape of Good Hope	1562	First war of religion (civil war) in France
1515	French victory over Swiss at Marignano	1565	Malta withstands Turkish siege
1517	Luther's 95 theses begins Reformation	1566	Dutch revolt begins
1519	Charles V elected Holy Roman Emperor	1571	Battle of Lepanto
1521	Beginning of wars between Charles V and Francis I	1572	Massacre of St Bartholomew (of Protestants in France)
1525	Imperial victory at Pavia	1577–80	Drake's voyage round the world
1526	Battle of Mohacs: Turks conquer most of Hungary	1580	Philip II of Spain becomes King of Portugal
1527	Sack of Rome	1588	Defeat of Spanish Armada
1534	Henry VIII of England becomes head of English Church; break with Rome complete	1593	Henri IV of France returns to Catholicism
1540	Pope recognizes Jesuit order	1594	Henri IV enters Paris; end of French religious wars
1545–63	Council of Trent	1595	France at war with Spain
1547	Charles V defeats Lutheran princes at battle of Mühlberg	1598	Peace between France and Spain
1555	Peace of Augsburg ends religious wars in Empire. Abdication of Charles V	1604	Peace between England and Spain
		1609	Truce: effective Spanish recognition of Dutch independence

GLOSSARY

Amenities   Comforts and conveniences.

Archivist   Person who looks after the records of another person or institution.

Autocratic   Dictatorial.

Baroque   The highly emotional and spectacular style characteristic of much European art between the late sixteenth and early eighteenth century.

Bishopric   Area in which a bishop exercises his authority.

Calvinist   Protestant follower of Jean Calvin.

Camerata   Group of musicians in Florence who invented opera.

Canon Law   Body of laws made by the Catholic Church for the government of the Church and its members.

Chivalry   Code of conduct of the Middle Ages, which governed the behaviour of nobles and knights.

Controversialist   Someone who causes arguments and debates.

Counter-Reformation   Movement of reform in the Catholic Church in response to Protestantism.

Dominican   Member of the Dominican order of friars, named after St Dominic.

Duchy   Territory ruled by a duke.

Feudal System   Organization of society into groupings such as barons, knights and serfs (see below) during the Middle Ages.

Galleon   Sailing ship suitable for ocean voyages which replaced the galley (see below).

Galley   Ship propelled by oars and sails, widely used in the Mediterranean Sea.

Heretic   Christian who champions doctrines contrary to the beliefs of his Church. Catholics regarded Protestants as heretics, and vice versa.

Hierarchy   System of organization by grades, one above the other, as practiced in the feudal system, for example.

Huguenot   French Protestant.

Humanism   A cultural movement of the Renaissance, based on classical studies.

Index   List of books which Catholics were forbidden to.own or read.

Inquisition   Catholic tribunal which investigated heresy.

Knights of St John   Religious order which also developed into a formidable military organization.

72

Laity   Members of a church who are not priests.

Landlubberly   Word used by sailors to describe a non-sailor.

Lutherans   Christians who follow the Protestant doctrines of Martin Luther.

Mannerist   Showy style of art that followed the Renaissance style.

Matchlock   Device that caused a spark when a trigger was pulled, igniting the gunpowder in an arquebus or other weapon.

Maxims   Brief general statements.

Mediator   Person who intervenes between two parties, to help them come to an agreement.

Obsolete   Out of date, or no longer effective.

Orthodoxy   The correct or proper set of beliefs, for example within a Church.

Pamphleteer   A writer of short argumentative booklets intended to win over readers to a particular religious or political point of view.

Paradoxical   A statement which seems to contradict itself, but in fact does not.

Picaresque   Describes a story in which the main character (usually something of a rascal) goes through a series of adventures.

Protestant Reformation   Revolt against the abuses in the Catholic Church which led to separate Protestant churches being established.

Rhetoric   Forceful writing which aims to sway the emotions rather than convince by rational argument.

Serf   A peasant within the feudal system (see above) who had a holding of land in return for working for his lord and giving part of his produce to him.

Sonnet   A fourteen line poem, originally Italian; there are famous English sonnets by Shakespeare, and others.

Speculation   Financial dealings based on hopes of profit to be made in the future.

Utopia   An imaginary perfect society. The word is taken from Sir Thomas More's book *Utopia*.

Vernacular   The ordinary spoken language of a country.

War of attrition   A war in which each side tries to wear the other down rather than overwhelm it in decisive battles.

FURTHER READING

Burckhardt, Jacob *The Civilization of the Renaissance in Italy* (Phaidon, 1981)

Chamberlin, E. R. *Everyday Life in Renaissance Times* (Batsford, 1965)

Green, V. H. H. *Luther and the Reformation* (Batsford/New English Library, 1964)

Habsburg, Otto von *Charles V* (Weidenfeld, 1967)

Harris, Nathaniel *The Age of Shakespeare* (Hamlyn, 1971)

Harris, Nathaniel *Spotlight on Elizabethan England* (Wayland, 1985)

Helm, P. J. *History of Europe 1460–1660* (Bell, 1961)

Koenigsberger, H. G., and Mosse, George L. *Europe in the Sixteenth Century* (Longmans, 1968)

Montgomery, Viscount *A History of Warfare* (Collins, 1968)

Ortiz, Antonio Domínguez *The Golden Age of Spain 1516–1659* (Weidenfeld, 1971)

Phillips, M. M. *Erasmus and the Northern Renaissance* (English University Press, 1950)

Seward, Desmond *Prince of the Renaissance* (Francis I) (Constable, 1973)

Wedgwood, C. V. *William the Silent* (Cape, 1944)

Original sources
Most of the writings mentioned in the text are widely available in paperback; for example, translations of Camoes, Castiglione, Cellini, Cervantes, Machiavelli, Montaigne, More, Rabelais and Vasari have all appeared in Penguin.

PICTURE ACKNOWLEDGEMENTS

The illustrations were supplied by: Ann Ronan Picture Library 8, 40, 55, 61, 63, 66; BBC Hulton Picture Library 12, 13, 31, 37; The British Museum 57; ET Archive Ltd 23, 32; Alan Langford 7; The Mansell Collection 5, 6, 10, 14, 17, 21, 26, 27, 28, 29, 34, 42, 43, 44, 48, 51, 53; Mary Evans Picture Library 18, 33, 38, 54, 60, 70; The National Gallery *front cover*; Malcolm Walker 25. The remaining pictures are from the Wayland Picture Library.

INDEX

Alberti, Leon Battista 18
Alexander VI, Pope 35
Arquebus, invention of 41–3

Bosch, Hieronymous 50
Brahe, Tycho 69
Breughel, Pieter 50
Burckhardt, Jacob 4, 9

Calvin, Jean 36, 38
Caravaggio 52
Castiglione, Baldassare 19, 68
Catholic Church 7, 8, 10, 32,
    35–6, 39
Caxton, William 55
Cervantes, Miguel de 47, 56
Charles V, Emperor 23–6, 27,
    28, 36, 41, 51, 64
City-states 11–13, 27
Columbus, Christopher 10
Copernicus, Nicolaus 69, 70
Council of Trent 39
Counter-Reformation 10, 32,
    39–40, 52, 60

Donatello 20, 21
Drake, Sir Francis 45, 46
Durer, Albrecht 50, 51

El Greco 52, 53
Elizabeth I, Queen of England
    30–31
Erasmus, Desiderius 20, 54, 56

Fashion 67–8
Ferdinand of Aragon 23
Florence 11–13, 15

Francis I, King of France 22–4,
    27

Gama, Vasco da 64, 65
Giotto 4, 20
Gunpowder, invention of 10, 41

Habsburg family 25, 27, 28,
    29–31
Henri IV, King of France 31
Henry VIII, King of England 22,
    23, 45
Hilliard, Nicholas 50, 52
Holbein, Hans 50
Holy Roman Empire 24, 28, 36
Hugenots 31
Humanists 16, 19–20, 54, 68

Isabella of Castille 23

Julius II, Pope 35

Knights of St John 47
Knox, John 36, 39

Lepanto, Battle of 47
Loyola, Ignatius 40
Luther, Martin 28, 32, 33, 35–7,
    67
Lutheranism 28, 36

Machiavelli, Niccolò 19, 56
Medici family 11, 15
Michelangelo 11, 48–50
Mirandola, Pico della 17–18
Monteverdi, Claudio 61
More, Sir Thomas 20, 56
Muhlberg, Battle of 41

Music 60–61

New Monarchies 22–3
New World 10, 24, 27, 64–5, 67–8

Ottoman Turks 46, 47

Palestrina, Giovanni da 50
Papal states 28, 35
Pavia, Battle of 27, 41
Peasants Revolt 67
Petrarch 4, 6, 11, 16
Philip II, King of Spain 22, 29–31, 43, 45, 65
Pilgrimage of Grace 67
Printing, invention of 10, 19, 55, 62
Protestant Reformation 7, 10, 32, 40
Ptolemaic theory 69–70

Rabelais, Francois 56
Raphael 5, 48

Sforza, Francesco 11
Seamen 31, 43, 44, 64–5
    English 31, 44
    Portuguese 44, 64–5
    Spanish 31, 44
Shakespeare, William 58
Society of Jesus 39–40
Spanish Armada 31, 45
Spenser, Edmund 58, 59

Tetzel, Johannes 34, 36
Titian 52
Trade, growth of 9–11, 63–6

van Eyck, Jan 52
Vernacular literature 10, 56
Veronese, Paolo 52
Vesalius, Andrea 68–9
Vinci, Leonardo da 11, 48

Warfare 41–7
Wars of religion 30, 35, 43